Love Poems...

Sunday Afternoons

E. Gene Givens

CITIOFBOOKS, INC.
3736 Eubank NE Suite A1
Albuquerque, NM 87111-3579
www.citiofbooks.com
Hotline: 1 (877) 389-2759
Fax: 1 (505) 930-7244

Ordering Information:

Quantity sales. Special discounts are available on quantity purchases by corporations, associations, and others. For details, contact the publisher at the address above.

Printed in the United States of America.

ISBN-13:   Softcover   979-8-89391-698-0

Library of Congress Control Number: 2025910532

Love Poems...

Sunday Afternoons

E. Gene Givens

CITI OF
BOOKS

DEDICATION

I:
even though . . .
your travels may be limited
your surroundings are full of adventure
seek them out and experience their passion

II:
even though . . .
we can possess love
but we cannot make love
without someone else's love

III:
even though . . .
loving someone
is not the same as
being *"in love"* with someone
enjoy the sensation, the pain
the insecurity, and the challenge
of discovering the difference

IV:
even though . . .
life is uncertain
live each day
with each day in mind . . .
there may not come another
so, smile, be nice
and love one another

Sunday Afternoons

POEM XVI: SUNDAY AFTERNOON

gray sky . . .
tried to sleep
couldn't
thought i'd get up
and cook
thought again
decided i shouldn't

rain . . .
nothing on tv
john wayne re-runs
just don't do
nothing for me

still raining . . .
you called
we talked
and i emptied
a bottle of wine
not noticing

ever since that
sunday afternoon
when it rains
i can't think of
anything
but you

SUITORS

you have cast many suitors aside
the many who have been mesmerized by
your style . . . your smile . . .
your eye . . .
they seek some secret thing
as if on a holy quest
some object or trophy to possess

many have spoken eloquent words
of adoration and love
only to fall silently to the ground . . .
unremembered

others have spoken impressive words of
self-importance and confidence
but their words too have gone unheard

many have spoken words
to entice, capture, and possess your spirit
but their effort have also failed
they were not the words
your heart longed to hear

why do they persist? . . .
no one knows the unknowable
you are like the elements
your spirit moves like the wind
and slips through their fingers like sand
you are like water that flows on forever
you cannot be captured or tamed . . .
at least . . .
not for long

LIKE THAT OLD MASON JAR . . .

i was empty
like that old mason jar
in the fruit cellar
i needed an illusion
something comforting
like an old quilted blanket
something warm, soft, and smooth
to the touch
something reassuring
like sunshine after a raging storm
i needed to feel protected
like a child protects
an ice cream cone
i needed something simple
as simple as a child's imagination
i needed to re-discover *'things'*
with an innocent ear and fresh eyes
i needed — wanted
to believe that romance
and passion
was still possible
that two people could still care
for one another
and that love was somewhere
out there
patiently waiting . . .
just like that old mason jar
in the fruit cellar

UNCONDITIONALLY

we met at the assemblage point
to discuss and admire
each other's
ethereal qualities
we went through all the
in/appropriate rituals
(as we had been taught to do)
while we exchanged
intrinsic views and values
i released you from your guilt
and you . . . mine
you discovered your strengths
and the difference between
being alone
and being lonely
while i rediscovered the joy
of doing nothing . . .
together
and the peace of giving
someone friendship . . .
unconditionally

FASCINATED BY MY SKIN

fascinated by my skin
you decided to climb in

no – not tonight i mused
i was tired . . . tired of being used

noticing my distance
you became slow, methodical
and persistent
        (not used to being refused)
maybe some conversation
a drink, and a dance
might lead to romance

so we danced
you talked . . . i listened
and took a chance

in the rain we walked to a breakfast date
even though, you kept reminding me
        (and yourself)
that you had to go, it was getting late

to my surprise, you were loud and rude
but that was only a façade, to protect
what was sensitive, soft, and smooth

the moment was brief
tender
yet, intense
and i have thought of nothing since . . .
since you became . . . fascinated
with my skin
and decided to climb in

JUST YOU . . .
(For Cindy)

i don't remember the exact moment
when i knew that i loved you
maybe, it was when i first saw you
as you slowly sashayed through the door
possibly, it was the way you
'looked like money'
in those fabulous clothes that you wore
or was it your sophisticated talk
that came along with that sophisticated walk
perhaps, it was when we first met
and i kissed your hand
because i thought you had to be *'special'*
maybe, it was your beautiful, radiant eyes
or possibly, it was just your gorgeous smile
that left me beguiled
could it have been the trust you displayed
or was it the respect you showed
and the laughter you made
or was it simply the support, empathy
and loyalty you gave
perhaps, it was the way you kissed me –
long . . . wet . . . and deep
or, maybe, it was when i watched you
as you laid fast asleep
or possibly . . . maybe . . . perhaps . . .
it was just timing . . . destiny . . . fate
that made me give you my heart
or maybe, it was just . . . you
that made me love you
from the very start

SINCE I MET YOU . . .

since i met you
i have found myself *"seeing"* . . .
seeing and feeling
all things anew . . .
you give 'sexy' a new meaning
you bring a fresh insight to the pleasures
joys, and callous pains, i felt before

i know, you just wanted me to see sparks instead but
without knowing it
you have made me so aware of *'things'* about myself
that i see in you
some things better . . .
some things less

i know, you just wanted me to be happy
but you bring a natural aura
of unembellished excitement with your smile
as you talked of your childhood dreams
me . . .
well, i just wanted to comfortable

i know, you had seen all the movies
and read all the books, from Dr. Sagan to Dr. Ruth
so, you wanted to embark on new journeys
of the exotic and fantastic

you knew your destination, and how, where, and
why you wanted to go there
and i was just recovering from journeys of my own
but . . . since i met you
i have found myself seeing . . .
seeing and feeling
all things anew . . .
on this journey with you

YOU REMIND ME . . .

when you presented your hand
a deep and a respectful bow was made
i caressed it gently and graced it with a kiss
then your eyes met mine
and my soul became fixed
you asked, *"what fixes your gaze, kind sir?"*
and my reply, with my life at risk:
you, my Queen . . . you . . .

you remind me of winter mornings – fresh and crisp
of green mountain pastures that rest just below the mist
of cool summer breezes
blowing across a smooth gentle sea
of infinite mathematics
universal happiness – squared
then cubed, to the nth degree

you my queen . . . you . . .
you remind me of . . . beautiful ballads – written
yet unsung
of brilliant sunsets when the day is done
of majestic kingdoms
and of adventurers bold
of the electric excitement felt
when a new journey unfolds
of a tender flower yet to bloom
of warm summer nights
under a bright yellow moon
of romantic poetry written
for the innocent of heart
of the emptiness felt
when two lovers' part

YOU REMIND ME . . .
(Continued)

my Queen . . .
as i kneel humbly at your feet
with my eyes imprisoned by your presence
by skin so soft . . . so supple . . . so sweet
my senses
are intoxicated with your essence
and my soul
is so full of what perfection should be
i must remind myself
that in my travels
i have seen beauty
but none could match
or eclipse the beauty of thee

for you, my Queen, you . . .
are the personification of perfection
your authority, dignity, and reputation
can never be diminished
no matter how long
and intense the search
one could not find fault
or even a blemish

for you, my Queen . . . you . . .
you remind me of love . . .
love unfinished

INTELLECTUAL PERCEPTIONS

be sympathetic to my
intellectual perception
of beauty
i have only read
of such things but now . . .
i see you
and no word
written or spoken
could ever
do you justice

TWO LOVERS

the night
with its thousand eyes
secretly watched
as two lovers
kissed
while the moon
nervously hid her face
behind the passing
clouds
then blushed full
to show her approval

TRANSITIONS

even in the womb our
bodies knew when it
was time
to move on
to new beginnings
it seems to be the
natural order of things
to grow out
of one's self
into another
but sometimes it's hard
even impossible
and sometimes
it goes unnoticed
so routine
as if it was the
natural order of things
to grow out
of one's self
into another

THE FACE OF SPRING

the first day of spring came
but the weather did not change
it seemed like this phenomenon
was definitely quite strange
instead of sunshine
there was wind, clouds, and rain

days passed
instead of flowers blooming
his worries and concerns grew
he asked himself
"what great thing was God up to?"

there must be a reason
for things happening this way
*"why would God do this to this season
or this day?"*

but the next day
the flowers began to bloom
all around the place
then he remembered
today was her birthday
and that spring
had been waiting for her
before it could even show its face

SUNDAY AFTERNOON SMILE

i have always enjoyed
sunday afternoons
people take time-out
to leave you alone
on sunday afternoons

people play jazz
and get tired
of being sick and tired
on sunday afternoons

where do people go
on sunday afternoons
in their sunday
morning clothes
strutting and smiling
their sunday afternoon smile

phones don't ring
hometown stores don't open
gas stations don't pump
and the abc stores are closed
on sunday afternoons

i love to sleep late
lay in bed and read the paper
listening to jazz
smiling and laughing
at your funny stories
and making love with you
especially
in the quite
of sunday afternoons

SEEDS

those seeds that you
dropped
into the flower bed
of my mind
have began to grow
some have blossomed
passers by marvel
an comment
on my green thumb
they ask me
"what's your secret?"
i just smile
and say
a little patience
a lot of love
a pinch of time
and you

SUBDUED

my heart was beating
with the speed of
hummingbird wings
as i melted with anticipation
deep within
primeval thoughts
subdued
any civilized notion
of sophistication
and like a reed
in a winter storm
i quivered at your touch
until i was covered
with silent rapture

LISTEN TO MY HEART

i have shared
and possessed
many hearts and souls
at least
that is what
i've been told
but no heart
that i have possessed
or shared
has compelled me to want
or linger
long enough
for us to grow old
together
i was just looking
for a vessel
to store my love in
and then
you came
and lent me
your heart
i listened
when your heart told me
that your love
was just enough
to fill my cup
not too much
but just enough . . .
for me

PHANTOM

fingers, soft and smooth
slowly making their way
from the tip of your toes
to the bottom of your feet
around your ankles
up your lower legs
resting at your inner thighs
as you catch your breath
contemplating
the next moment
. . . the next move
wondering if those fingers
would go any further . . .
in the right direction
. . . then you wake up
from a dream so real . . .

so, if you every feel
that someone
is softly stroking
and gently loving you
it's me
making sweet love to you
in my mind
with my heart
and all of my being

WAVE TRAIN

i can feel the wave begin
like ripples on a pond
radiating
in concentric circles
around . . . over . . .
through . . . me
making flesh walk
and hair stand on end
a never-ending wave train
of excitement
tenderness
trust and joy
with your every touch
i can feel each wave
peak
then begin again
rolling
like satin silk sheets
in a cool summer wind

THE DEPTH OF REAL LOVE

the depth of real love
cannot be measured
in inches, grams, or ounces

no, it cannot it be measured
by some invisible measuring cup
of time

nor can the depth of real love
be measured
by the number of smiles, sex, or a kiss
nor can it be measured
by how often one is missed

once real love is given
it will last forever
it cannot die

real love will always make room
for itself
and occupy a space in your heart
even though
you may be with another soul
today

real love will always exist
in your heart
in your mind
and in the ether of your memories
until your dying day

SEARCH

i search and search
for the right words
to describe
my perception
of the feelings
i have for you
and it's funny
how i always seem
to find them
bouncing off the wall
of my heart

LITHOGLYPH

tho time and space
separates our bodies
your figure
your motion
your words remain
etched . . . engraved
in my mind
in my heart
and in my soul

DECADENT NUBIAN DESSERT

conversations between the two of us
was like making and eating a decadent dessert . . .
with our fingers
"wouldn't you agree?" she inquired
yes . . . i do, was my initial reply . . .

but then again . . . i mused to myself
i have always thought of her as a
delicious and tempting treat
like a Decadent Nubian Dessert . . .
a chocolate cake - hot, gooey, delicious, and sweet
like taking a bite of a dense chocolate truffle
or maybe a scrumptious chocolate cheesecake
with its own unique, smooth, and creamy
texture that yields only luscious mouthwatering flavors
chocolate . . . deep, dark, rich, and sweet

people say . . . *real* chocolate
generates a true feeling of bliss
and it is always delicious
even when nibbled right out of the package

but . . . a word of caution to all who reads
making fancy chocolate desserts requires
dexterity, patience, and concentration
but if making a Decadent Dessert . . .
it is one that cannot be helped but to
slowly enjoy the mixing, then savor the flavors
especially, a Decadent Nubian Dessert
a dessert that can exceed all your wants
satisfy all of your needs
and meet all your expectations

POEM XII (LAST NIGHT)

last night
we made passionate
love
and your body
was like a generator
producing volts of
electricity
currents
flowed
through my body
stimulating
my mind
making my nerves
stand on end
giving birth
to my soul

POEM XIII (AROMA)

the sweet aroma
you left
on my sheets
only made me realize
how empty
my life
really is

SINLESS LOVERS

when we were young
and so full of virtue
we gave without asking
and accepted without acknowledgment
your innocent eyes
and the soul of motown
made life so simple . . . so sweet
as we held hands
and each other
as we danced slow and close
under blue lights in steamy basements

when we were young . . .
just being near you
just hearing your soothing voice
was the only answer – nothing else mattered
because you were mine
and i was yours . . . forever
and that was enough

when we were young . . .
everything was so clear – so transparent
there was nothing worth hiding
we just stripped off the flesh
so, the bones would show
leaving nothing but two sinless lovers
who were artless and pure
yet, so intense with the intent to please
. . . each other

ENCHANTED

often
when i'm feeling this way
and am totally relaxed
i am flooded with thoughts of you
no moment of mine
is safe from you
you invade my mind
indiscriminately
no matter where i am
what i am doing
or who i am with
and this is not incomprehensible
to me
for i fully understand
why
i am so mesmerized
by the essence of you

A PERFECT MATCH

your hand in mind
synchronized heart beats
complimenting thoughts
your jokes
my laughter
and the joyful
silence
when we do
nothing
together

THE ITALIAN LOVER

come hold me
and fold me like a baker
making exotic italian pastries
for his secret love

come hold me
and fold me like the gentle fingers
of a loving italian grandmother
as she adds her secret ingredients
and folds and rolls the dough
for her special tortellini pasta
and her delicious little sfogliatelle

come hold me
and fold me in your bosom
like dew drops
that gather and swell
when caught in the petals
of a lily's bell

come hold me
and fold me in your arms
and never let me go
don't you know that
i love you so much
that my heart aches continuously
when i am so far away
only you
can provide the relief that i need

come hold me
and fold me in your love . . .
and in your heart . . .
and never let me go

SILENT COMPANION

with you
my heart walks
that may mean nothing
to you
but it's still there
just the same
casually strolling alone
disguised
as you shadow

POEM V: A SONG

i attempted
to write you
a song
using the air
as my music
i messed up
and it came out
as a poem
that only
my heart
could sing

COME GROW OLD WITH ME

come grow old with me
as we walk through
the corridor of eternity
on our way to and from the galaxies
the hallways may get dark
but our love will be our radiant torch

SOULMATES

since the day they met
they had been adoring, affectionate
devoted, tender, and kind to each other

and over the years, they had learned
and had demonstrated
that they were both
'precious' and *'special'* people
although, they may not have admitted it
they both believed that the other was a treasure
a person of great value
someone that was not to be wasted
or treated carelessly

so, at the end, before it was too late
it was only fittingthattheystarted
to acknowledge their appreciation
for each other
for the years of supplying laughter love
encouragement, and emotional support
to each other, and their families
and for being a treasure
in their own fashion
someone who had been a precious jewel
to each other's soul
someone who had been a fellow traveler
on their journey through life
in the end . . .
they both realized
that they were just soulmates
to each other

EVERY ONCE IN A WHILE

seeing you in person
looking into your eyes
talking to you on the phone
or exchanging an email
reveals different aspects
about you . . .
your personality . . . me

sometimes
i never really know how you feel
because you're so elusive

every once in a while
i get to experience . . . see . . .
and hear your real thoughts
and what you're really thinking

often
it feels like i'm in the dark
and have no clue where you are . . .

at other times
i feel satisfied
that you seem to be happy
and that you want to be
right where you're supposed to be
. . . right here with me

SOME JOURNEYS MAY TAKE LONGER . . .

there are times . . .
times when i can remember
how intoxicated i would become with the sight of you
the tenderness of your touch, and how it made my flesh walk
how i tried to take deep breaths whenever you were near
trying to drown my senses with the fragrance of you

and there are times . . .
times when i can taste your very essence
anticipate your every move
think your every thought
mouthing each word before it was spoken

and then there are times . . .
times when your spirit seemed so far away . . .
traveling . . . searching . . . discovering . . .
times when my chest could not find air
and my soul felt lost without you

stubbornly, i admit to myself
that i must learn to be patient . . .
from time to time
everyone must go on their own "special" journey
perhaps, some journeys are meant to be taken alone
i guess it's true what they say

> *some journeys*
> *may take longer than others*
> *while some will take no time at all*
> *yet, some journeys are never finished*

is this one of those times
one of those *'special'* kind of journeys?
a journey without notice . . . without direction
a journey without destination . . . without purpose
a journey without . . . me?

HOUSEKEEPING: Sunday 3:37 p.m.

it started to rain, and i decided to shuffle
some papers around . . . and move some clothes
from one place to another
this process is what is called *'housekeeping'*
or *'straightening up'* one's mess

it rained, and i thought about all the things i needed to do
and why i hadn't done them . . .
i told myself that, *"i must learn to exhibit more discipline in
dealing with my personal affairs"*

it rained, and the sky grew dark, and i thought about
an old friend, and how we said goodbye . . .

me – trying to be cool like some character i'd seen

you – trying to make your cosmopolitan entrance like you
saw someone do on a movie screen

neither one of us really paying much attention to one
another
. . . not until we started to walk towards that last gate

. . . when i went through that finalgate,iheard
"i'm gonna miss you," slip from your lips

. . . as i walked to the plane, we grew father and farther
apart, and i heard a distant voice say
"you better call me this time!"
"o.k.?"
"do you hear me?"
"hurry back!"
. . . i just turned and nodded, afraid to open my mouth
because i knew that this would be our last goodbye

I COULD HAVE LOVED YOU FOREVER

when we were young
loving you was easy
and dreams were there just for the taking
but that was yesterday
and dreams don't always come true
i loved you so much
until it hurt
this i know
because my heart told me so
i could have spent my whole life loving you
but the future offered uncertain choices
and there seemed to be no safe path for us
so i learned how to hide my feelings
even when i loved you so
and when we looked into tomorrow
fear and doubt were the loudest voices
 and only empty choices remained
i didn't want to go
but i just couldn't stay
i could have loved you . . .
forever
because loving you was so
easy but that was yesterday
and i just couldn't stay

JUST A PART...

i have always been there for you
i just wanted to help you
find your place in the world
but you just couldn't see . . .

deep inside
you knew my love was true
i just wished that you had loved me
enough to love me beyond
your doubts . . . your fears . . . your regrets

i would risk my life to touch you again
i just wished that you didn't regret
the stolen moments we shared . . .
the smiles . . . the laughter . . . the bliss

when i think about it . . .
i know i loved you . . .
more than life itself
the fact is . . .
i have always loved you
even though you can't say the same

you were just stuck . . . always looking
at things from/in your past
instead of looking at . . . seeing
what was right in front of you

and now . . .
i am just a part of your past . . .
a memory . . .
and you are just a part
of mine

SHE SAYS . . .

she says . . .
that she still loves him
because he was the only one . . .
the only one
that kept their promise
the promise to come back for her
out of fear, she says . . .
with regret
she chose to stay and suffer
to not follow her heart
and leave with him
the one, she says . . .
she will love
. . . forever

FLAMING RAINBOWS

frosted panes
steaming mugs of hot chocolate
and chamomile tea
old memories
of how we liked to chill

you painted pictures of ecstasy in my mind
with your loving words and the way we spent
rainy fall sunday afternoons watching the leaves fall

i liked going to bed in the early darkness
so we could catch each other's dreams

we were just stubborn late blooming lovers
that complimented the flaming rainbow of colors
that precede its death

. . . it was just a wonderful optical illusion anyway

my plant died today, and i thought of how, each year
i watched the trees shed their flaming colors in the fall
until they were empty and bear
and how they grew stronger
from the rain, during the following spring

you know . . .
the changing seasons always remind me
of how long you've been gone
and how our love grew
then blossomed
and how it radiated
like a flaming rainbow
just before it died

ALL OF ME

all of me
wants all of you
don't leave me out in the cold
remember . . .
you once loved all of me too
before i made those painful choices
not to call . . .
not to see . . .
not to go . . .
not to be . . .
with you
i'm sorry i didn't believe in you
sorry for making those choices
don't you still have feelings for me?
or has time closed the doors to your heart
and your heart does not beat for me
as it once did
if i could just see you again
i could explain . . .
i'm ready now
to give you all of me

EVEN LOVERS

even lovers need to get away
vacation
holiday
just a short visit or stay
it makes no difference
what excuse is used
to get away
after all
is said and done
they love you
the same old way
for being there
when they didn't need
a vacation
holiday
short visit or stay
or any other kind of excuse
they used to get away

HONDURAS: In The Aguan Valley

here
in the Aguan Valley
surrounded by the mountains of God
the sun . . . the heat . . . the humidity
gives no quarter
the night comes early
the stars shine with a brilliance
and the river flows quietly
while he, like the tropical creatures
sit and watch the day surrender his thrown
feeling empty . . . power – less . . .
no telephone . . . and alone
here
in the Aguan Valley wishing . . .
wishing for things taken for granted
simple things, like the love they shared . . .
the love she had given him . . .
places . . . moments . . . events . . .
all taken for granted
simple things
that he did not take full advantage of
or take the time to see . . .
alone . . .
power – less . . . no telephone . . .
the mountains . . . the stars . . .
and her so far away . . .
and him . . . sitting there in the dark
on the banks of the river
in the Aguan Valley
15 degrees from the equator . . .
with an aching in his heart

WAITING . . .
FOR HER WOUNDS TO HEAL

through the daise, she heard them say
"she'll look just like new when they're finished...
"this kind of injury is commonplace these days" . . .
she was told that she must remain still
or her wounds won't heal properly . . .

the doctors can stitch and patch up
the abrasions contusions, cuts, and traumas
but who would tend to the deep cuts
and gashes that were beyond the senses . . . time?

in the beginning, she wanted to be fair, honest, and
trusting, hoping that those intangibles would be
returned in kind, but instead, only doubt, deceit and
duplicity were the benefits of her labor . . .
yes, labor, because she "worked" at it . . .
worked harder and longer
than she had ever worked at anything in her life

at each confrontation
the compelling charm of his appearance, his smile
was so overwhelmingly disarming that she eagerly
waited for the smallest sign of sincerity
and that is what he gave her
just a small sign . . .
because he knew, that was all she needed

she often wondered . . .
if she was caught up in her own self-importance
as if he owed her something for loving him . . .

WAITING . . .
FOR HER WOUNDS TO HEAL
(Continued)

even now, while her body was numb with pain
she continued to search for explanations / excuses

but this time, when he came to visit
things seemed to be different
the questions and answers were not clouded
with the aesthetics of his cologne
and his rugged good looks . . .
this time, it was different . . .
the bland smell of alcohol and medicines
and the monotone atmosphere
that makes people speak in quite voices
plus the harshness of the cold gray sky outside . . .
stood watching

he was only there for just a few short moments
but it seemed like hours
as they shared a non-conversation with their eyes
he seemed to be so out of his element
there were no other garments, music, cars, or visual
aids at his disposal, to enhance his presentation
other than his plain, white, paper, hospital gown
and a mask that hid his face . . .

out of his element, and feeling uncomfortable
he left . . .
his footsteps echoed though the silence
leaving her feeling empty, once again
waiting . . . and wondering . . . how long
would it take . . . for 'all' of her wounds to heal?

RAINDROPS . . .

it rained . . .
rained great big raindrops
and i wondered
how much love
could each one of them hold

it rained . . .
and i thought about
all the lies you told
and all the lies that
i actually listened to

it rained . . .
and i thought about
the different lies you told
and the many different reasons
i gave myself for believing them all

last night i cried . . .
cried great big teardrops
and i wondered
how much love
did each one of them hold

ROOMS IN MY HEART

i'm sorry
i was young, angry, poor, and out of control
i was immature
and my behavior was simply wrong
i know i should have acted better
and i know you must have felt hurt
after i said those things to you
your friends told me
that you cried for days
i apologize . . .
i'm so sorry that i took
all those negative things out on you
i was just scared of your love
it was the first time for me
and i didn't think i could measure up
i felt i didn't deserve a love like yours
a love so precious and so pure
many moons have passed
and we have lived
many lives of our own
only the pictures remain
i hope you still have room in your heart
to forgive me
because
i have seen all the faces of love
but only one still remains
and i hope you still have a place
in your heart for me
because i have many rooms
of love in my heart
waiting for you

OFFERS

they all had offers:
Trice said she was alone, lonely, and looking
but she was too selective
and refused the few offers she had

Pearl said she was alone, lonely, and unhappy
but she was too particular
and refused the few offers that she had

Pat said she was alone, and lonely
but she had fifty offers
and she eagerly turned them
all down all except for a few
because of their appearance, money
or lack of material goods

Pat later said that she had felt desperate
and was happy that they had asked
and if she accepted the offers
that the dates would be amazing . . .
they would be exciting . . .
and she would become an
'active woman'
and be treated in the ways and lifestyles
that she had wanted to become accustomed to
she would be envied and admired by all
so, she accepted the offers
and went on several dates
and ended up in a several relationships
she was finally treated in the ways and lifestyles
that she had wanted to become accustomed to

in the end, they all regretted their choices
but only one ended up unhappy, alone
and lonely, with someone else

A SEASON OF WAITING

like the rhythm of the seasons
trees always change colors
showing their emotions . . .
the joy of spring . . . the happiness of summer . . .
the beauty of fall . . . and the bleakness of winter
with each winter season, the days grew shorter
and the stars shone brightly in the night sky

down below, a temporary season of wilderness
and waiting had captured the imagination
and every sigh was a sigh of loneliness
while every heart break still brought another
unwanted tear

as they anxiously wait for a new season . . .
a new beginning
a new season of excitement
where they didn't have to fear the loneliness
a season where they could trust and believe again
a season where true hearts could thrive
a new season where hope and love would be out there
waiting to turn their night into day
waiting to set their hearts free . . .
free to enjoy the joys of spring

and with that new season, only then would they know
that it was ok to begin again
free to be anything that love wanted them to be
only then could they seek and find
someone who would break through the clouds
and make them smile that crescent smile
and make their heart sing anew . . .
sing as happily as the birds of spring

EXPERT LOVERS

as experts
they tried to teach
each other
(like most lovers do)
what little each of them knew
about respect and friendship
and a love that was true
most things
both already knew
and a few
they discovered on their own
while sitting, waiting, and wondering
all alone
checking their empty mail boxes
answering machines
and watching their silent telephones

HEAVY RAIN

golden oldies
soulful, slow, and sweet
echo and drift through the air
as memories . . .
memories of yesterday – and you
are stirred up
like dust particles
by a gentle wind
spinning, whirling, and twirling
only to settle at my feet . . .
a wish for rain
is my only thought – my only need
rain . . .
clear, fresh, and sweet
heavy rain . . .
heavy enough
to wash away these tears
these tears of joy and pain
that flow like rivers
in my memory
from my mind
through my eyes
and down my cheeks
rain . . . heavy rain
clear . . . fresh . . . and sweet

THE NATURE OF THINGS

it is the nature of things to survive
though some things fade into nothingness . . .
unremembered

Steve did not know the depth of Gail's pain
although, at times, he felt its individuality
its emptiness . . .
its wrath . . .
even now, he remembers

Steve did not know the depth of Gail's hurt
nor could he measure her frustrations . . .
he was just a man
so, from the silent shadows
he would watch her eyes well with tears
and feel helpless

it was during those moments
that Steve tried to comfort Gail
not knowing if that was what she needed . . .
or wanted . . .
or if that would be enough

but this time
as Steve and Gail
rested in each other's arms
their silence was broken
as she gently caressed his face
and said . . .
"i'll be alright,"
"it's the nature of things to survive"

THE NATURE OF THINGS
(Continued)

another tear feel to her cheek
as she slowly shook her head

"i lost another one," she said

Steve kissed her tears
and whispered in her ear

"don't worry, we'll try again"

Gail just looked Steve in his eyes
and smiled
as another tear fell to her cheek
and the thought . . . the words
"you're just a man, you'll never understand"
almost passed her lips

at that moment Gail felt alone . . .
frustrated . . .
empty . . .
sad and angry . . .
but she also felt loved . . .
as Steve watched another tear fall to her cheek

ON BEING MARRIED: A PICNIC

being married to you
was like
carrying cement blocks
in a back-pack
or eating rocks and boulders
for an afternoon snack

ON SEPARATION/DIVORCE

now that you've left
with more
than your share
the weight
of life
is so much easier
to bear

I THOUGHT IT WOULD BE EASY

each time
i thought i could save them from their situation . . .
save them from themselves
i shared my visions and dreams with them
and they echoed those visions and dreams
as if they were similar . . .
as if they were compatible . . .
as if they were their own
i thought providing them with . . .
trust, support, security, my heart . . .
and me
that all of those things would be appreciated
and be returned in kind
and we would find happiness and love would bloom
coming from the projects
i thought we had something in common –
penniless, poor, ambitious
and a need to escape their condition
i thought i could help them
with their dreams and well-being
so, i thought we understood each other
and wanted the same things
it seemed, we were attracted to each other
like magnets
that were stuck together by the universe
but in the end . . . i was wrong
there was *"no our" "no us"* and *"no we"*
it was only *"i"*
"i think" "i want" and "i need" . . .

I THOUGHT IT WOULD BE EASY
(Continued)

and those echoes that i thought
were common visions and dreams
were really an echo of *"my"*
original visions and dreams
that they were reciting back to me
but their dreams were simple
and their visions were simple too
a simple vision and a simple dream
of escape
by any means necessary
it became evident that our true
magnetic characteristics
only caused our north poles
to eventually
repulse and push each other away
in order for either of us to survive . . .
to find our true direction . . .
to find our true north
i can remember the moment
they slowly disappeared
into the night
heading south, east, and west
with more than their own
while i was left
with broken pieces of myself
and a pocket full of bad pennies
that i thought . . .
it would be easy . . .
to get them to shine

CAMERA ROLL

she had passed through life
dealing with all the stresses and strife
that had been imposed upon her
she had developed photographic images of herself
where she had given little bits and pieces
like puzzle pieces
to everyone, but herself

her life seemed to be like a camera roll
in her mind, there were photos
of every defining moment
she could remember them all
like they were yesterday . . .
images so vivid . . . so real

sometimes . . . the images . . .
the views were distorted
possibly, by herself
or, maybe, by someone else
perhaps, she had moved in too close
or let them in her circle too soon

sometimes . . . she felt
that she had often went to the extreme
reckless and careless with her choices and dreams
she paid no heed to her inner voice
but now, she felt, she had learned
and she felt it was her turn
because she still wanted to be happy

CAMERA ROLL
(Continued)

she discovered that she had given her all
and there seemed to be nothing left
but everyone deserves to be happy, she thought
everyone deserves to laugh and cry, sometimes
to be hugged, kissed, wine and dined, sometimes
and now it was her turn, she thought
to truly be happy

in the end, she just wanted to be happy . . .
she thought of giving her all
once again
(as she had been taught to do)
in order for her to achieve her ultimate dream
it was the ultimate path to happiness
but now
she found that her soul was empty
with no more puzzle pieces left
she was only left with being content
once again
to look through her camera roll . . .
of the photographs of her life
and wish that she could be happy

ALMOST TOO COMFORTABLE

she had become content . . . satisfied . . .
almost too comfortable . . .
with being emotionally empty

she no longer had to consider
if, or how much, she wanted
or could give to another

she no longer concerned herself
with the how or why of it all
only the price to be paid for someone's
"i just want to get to know you"
or the oh so sincere
"i just want to share my life with someone special"
or the infamous salutation
"i love you"

she just wanted the bottom line . . .
the ultimate price
for someone wanting
to take so much of herself
from herself
without so much as a howdy-do
or a nice, and kind, please, and thank you

in this unique position
she doesn't have to issue or accept blame
wait . . . plead . . . or beg to be respected
loved or cared for
at last!
she no longer had to meet
anyone's expectation . . .
or they hers

ALMOST TOO COMFORTABLE
(Continued)

yes, it does seem that she had become
comfortable . . .
comfortable with being emotionally empty

she had become
more or less
a little too comfortable
so much so
that she almost felt happy . . .
happy that she no longer had to bear
all the weight
the weight of responsibility
for someone else's . . . *"stuff"*
like the perpetual airport porter
searching for, finding
and lugging around
everyone else's
lost emotional baggage

THE BROKEN ONES

they were thought to be broken –
physically, mentally, and spiritually
then they met someone . . .
someone who helped heal
their fractured parts
in all the right places
someone who and gave them strength
where there was none
gave them the strength
to take the next step
to look forward to a new day
with hope
to follow a new . . . no
to choose a different path

even though they knew better
they continued to make
some of the same mistakes
because some of their old/familiar ways
seemed to die hard

they had to learn what most people
seemed to ignore
that it was ok
to love, trust, and share
to let someone in
that relationships are a negotiation
and sometimes, you must be the
team captain or the band leader
instead of just a member

THE BROKEN ONES
(Continued 2 OF 3)

they also learned that there will always
be weak and damaged people out there
that just don't mean you well
you know, the ones that can't handle
the pressure of a relationship
the pressure of being honest with themselves
so, they try to siphon off
what is good and noble from your soul
and take all that they think they can steal
or misuse
in an attempt, to make themselves whole
always ending up with more than their share . . .
with more than what they could use

in time, they discovered
that you cannot remain bitter
and disappointed from your trials
that some dreams don't always come true
that you must help someone love you
because loving someone is hard
that the pendulum of love, peace, and justice
is always waiting
for demonstrations of honesty
kindness and righteousness

and they were eventually comforted
by the knowledge that hate, selfishness
and greed will never prosper

THE BROKEN ONES
(Continued 3 OF 3)

but most of all, that prayer changes things
and that hope, forgiveness, compassion . . .
and time
will always help one to endure
and to help the broken ones realize
that they were not broken
but simply unfinished . . .
and that they were just passing through
on their way . . .
to their next adventure . . .
to their next challenge . . .
to their next success

IF I COULD . . .

if i could . . .
i'd speak the words
that would make you understand
see and feel my pain . . . my regret . . .
my passion . . .
my need to love and to be loved in return
if i could . . . i would

i can tell you anecdotes, stories, limericks, and rhymes
that may cause you to smile and cry, from time to time
and maybe, now an then, if you have the mind
you'll reflect and reminisce about your own . . .
about how cruel and wonderful life can be
and how much you've grown

but, no matter how hard i try
i can not seem to find the right words
expressions or tone
the right words that will keep me from being alone . . .
words that would transport you to this place
a place where i wait to be discovered
this little out of the way place
where i wait for someone to fnd me . . .
a place where i wait for someone to love
for someone to see, understand, and truly love me
if i could only fnd the right words . . .

if i could . . . i really would

I CAN FEEL IT...

this texas sun burns deep
i can feel it . . .
it has begun
the bleaching of my bones

i can feel it . . .
a single bead of sweat
s-l-o-w-l-y
travelling down my spine . . .
evaporating

the hot harsh winds blisters my flesh
and suffocate my every breath
i can feel it . . .
the sandblasting of my soul

the cold desert night leaves me like ice
with only my hallucinations to warm me
i can feel it . . .
your water-sweet kisses upon my swollen
parched lips

my footprints disappearing
into a sea of sand
leaving no trail . . . no sign
for you to follow
i can feel it . . .

the distance
your absence
my emptiness
and how much i will miss you
i can feel it . . .

EPILOGUE: I AM A NOVEL

each one of my chapters
is a day in my life
Book I spills into Book II
and so on and so on
each chapter is comparable
to a paperback
like a fiction
that becomes non-fiction
for everyone that takes the time
to turn the pages
characters change
but constantly/always remaining
the same beginning from
within contending against the
end